The

Complete

Wo/Man:

An Index to the Heart

Marcia B. Armstead

Marcia B. Armstead

The Complete Wo/Man:
An Index to the Heart

Edited by
Olson Perry and Billy E. Wright

Copyright 2002 Marcia B. Armstead
ISBN 1-57258-231-6
Library of Congress Catalog Card No. 2002 104708

Write to:
The Complete Woman/Man Seminars
P. O. Box 17360
Colorado Springs, CO 80935-7360
marcia@complete-seminars.org
www.complete-seminars.org

Dedication

To the many seminar participants who have taken time out to attend presentations of **The Complete Woman/Man Seminars** in order to improve the quality of their lives.

To my life-long friends: Betty Anderson, Dianne Hampton, Darleen Simmonds, Carlyle B. Skinner, and Robert Smith.

Finally, to my younger sister, Clover Fleming, the most daring, provocative, and sensitive woman I have ever known.

To Carol + Henry

love,

marcia

4/11/04

Contents

Acknowledgments

I have been extremely blessed by God to preside over activities of **The Complete Woman/Man Seminars** for the past several years. It is a ministry that one does not do alone. Consequently, God has recruited a team of consultants to whom I am eternally grateful: Betty Anderson, Jackson Doggette, Jr., Kassie Dunmore, Yvonne Grimes, Betty Lee-Hogan, Esther Mateos, Karen Michael, Bettie Reynolds, and Donnette Dwyer-Williams. I thank them for caring, sharing, and encouraging.

Special thanks to Sylister and Ivory Jackson, and Ernest and Carmel Boger who kept me reminded that there is nothing impossible with God. Thanks to my sons, Eugene, for technical support and know-how, and Jonathan, for keeping my faith alive.

Most of all, I thank God for saving my life, accepting my repentance through the blood of Jesus Christ, and sending the Holy Spirit to empower me with His might.

The impetus for this book is my appreciation to God for healing me spiritually and physically. My promise to serve Him for the rest of my life is being fulfilled through this book, and **The Complete Woman/Man Seminars.** The Seminars has traveled throughout the United States and overseas where Christian consultants have addressed anyone who will listen, social support groups, Bible conferences, women's and men's retreats, educational institutions, churches, and businesses. My hope is that *this book* will be a help to others, and will travel where The Seminars may not go.

Foreword

In this era of fast-paced activities, the juggling of career and domestic responsibilities, and the ever increasing demands of everyday life—medical care, food, shelter, clothing, education—you sometimes have to stop and wonder where YOU are in the whole scheme of things. Who are you? Where are you headed? And, at what period did you manage to get yourself lost.

If your life has somehow become unglued, and you are searching for solution and satisfaction, *this volume* is for you. Its theme is a call to completeness in Christ Jesus, resulting in ultimate peace and happiness. This book is a compilation of experiences, events, and illustrations that depict the goodness of God toward those who love Him and the special blessings that are afforded to those who follow His commands.

The stories begin not where Marcia B. Armstead was born, but where she was reborn. Where she met God, felt His leading in her life, and experienced the joy of His will. Excerpts of her experiences have been told from time to time in her seminars but never before in writing.

Ms. Armstead shares not only her experiences, but stories of Biblical characters to whom many of her contemporaries can relate. These stories are recounted so the reader may understand that it does not matter how sordid or complex your past has been, God can renew your life if you turn it all over to Him.

By Roseita Browne

Chapter One
Personal Imaging, Part I

In the late 1970's, while our husbands were studying for their Masters of Divinity degree, my girlfriend, Betty, and I pursued ways to assist our families financially. So, because we had an affinity toward looking good at all times, we contracted with a garment manufacturer to sell clothing via private home showings. This we did on the weekends.

Amidst the challenges of full-time employment, rearing our children, and household chores, this second job was like a career. It was something we enjoyed and really looked forward to doing. After three years of one-on-one consulting and teaching young wo/men how to dress well, our husbands finally graduated. Our families moved to other cities; and though Betty and I stayed in close contact, we had not communicated with our former clients.

About a year after graduate school, I received an urgent telephone call. The caller was a young lady with whom we had consulted who had changed her entire appearance. She stated that she had been following our directives and dressing very professionally at work. Today, however, a male coworker approached her and eagerly wanted to know what had caused this change in her appearance. What was the secret? What has happened in her life to bring about such a change?

Today's dilemma was that my former client did not know how to respond. "Carol" did not know what to say.

She was void of a message behind her fashion statement. It was then that I knew *it was not enough to alter the exterior without renovating the interior.* I felt a personal guilt that suggested I had cheated this individual by placing maximum emphasis on the look rather than on the heart. After all, the complete look is *an index to the heart.* This caller seriously needed help and I had to do something for her. So, I promised to get back with her by evening.

Nothing But Leaves

I began my research by conducting a self-examination. Perhaps the answer to her problem could be gained by sharing with her **my** life-changing experiences. After all, I had come a long way from the antagonistic, self-centered, opinionated person I used to be. I now loved deeply, cared intensely, and forgave easily. At what point, I wondered, did this change take place?

It was hard to believe, but as I looked back on my life, and viewed the progression, I knew my inner beauty grew out of a spiritual refining process. The process began when I **fully** surrendered my life to the will of God. At first, I could not understand these new behaviors, this change, because I normally would strike out when things did not go my way, or when someone did not do or say something positive relating to our relationship.

However, after my full surrender to God, and my restoration to completeness, I came to clearly understand that friends can only give what they have to give and not what I want or expect of them. I am able to accept people for who they are, and what they are becoming in Christ Jesus. After all, no two minds think alike or will ever think alike. And, if there were no uniqueness, there would be no diversity.

So, though I may appear, to me, to be different in emotional responses to those whom I believe do not love, care, or forgive as I, we are all a part of the magical rainbow called humanity at its best.

BRAVO! Yet, I knew this self-assessment was not enough to help my friend. I had to give her something more profound, so I sought the help of God through prayer. After talking to our Father, I was led by the Holy Spirit to go to the real source for guidance--the Bible (**KJV**): Mark chapter 11:12-14 & 20.

> *And on the morrow, when they were come from Bethany, he [Jesus] was hungry:*
> *And seeing a fig tree afar off having leaves, he came, if haply he might find any thing thereon: and when he came to it, he found nothing but leaves for the time of figs was not yet.*
> *And Jesus answered and said unto it, No man eat fruit of thee hereafter for ever. And his disciples heard it.*
> *And in the morning, as they passed by, they saw the fig tree dried up from the roots.*

The fig tree looked attractive. Surely, Jesus thought it had fruit since it was natural for figs to appear before the leaves; so if there were leaves, there should be fruit. But, there was none. There was **nothing but leaves**. Jesus cursed the tree; it withered and died.

It was then that I knew the answer I had to give; not just to my friend that evening, but to all with whom we came in contact. Like the fig tree, *it is not enough to look good, but we must be good*, and be able to give an explanation of our position. This is what God requires.

The Bible warns against premature advertising. It encourages preparation of heart and understanding of purpose, so wo/men eager to display presence may also have content. The book of I Peter 3:15 says, "But sanctify the Lord God in your hearts; and be ready always to give an answer to every man that asketh you a reason of the hope that is in you with meekness and fear." The hope that is within you must be visible, and audible. And, **your message must always be as grand as your statement**.

God has clearly shown us in His word that no wo/man can be complete if s/he has the look (the form) and no power (no message). Therefore, if the appearance is **an index to the heart**, what does it say of the heart, or the mind? So, teach us, our seminar participants urge, a pattern of behavior that governs the heart and adds power to presence.

Learning to Walk before you Talk

All humans come into this world as babies. In natural childhood development, a baby walks before s/he talks. **Personal Imaging, Part I** is your listening, your understanding, and your *walking* with God. The complete wo/man reads, observes, and learns from the word of God how to walk. Like a new-born baby so is a born again Christian. You learn to crawl before you walk, and walk before you talk.

Because of sin, there are babies born with hearing impairments and speech impediments. Yet, with the invention of sign language, these individuals may, and do, occupy positions in the world of communications. Likewise, there are wo/men who are spiritually and morally impaired. Their grasp on the deep spiritual truths of the scriptures may not be as firm as others. Thus, it is my desire that these pages will aid wo/men in developing inward beauty and reaching a level of completeness in Christ Jesus. Colossians 2:9-10 states:

> *For in him dwelleth all the fullness of the Godhead bodily.*
> *And ye are **complete** in him, which is the head of all principality and power.*

Developing inward beauty--**learning to walk before you talk**--is like climbing a set of stairs, one step at a time. There are nine steps in this inward beauty process, and these are found in the Sermon on the Mount as outlined in Matthew 5:3-12, **The Beatitudes**.

Nine Steps Toward Modeling *Inward* Beauty

"Learning to *Walk* Before You *Talk*"

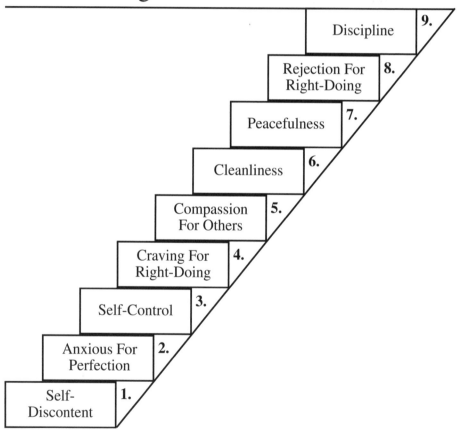

9. Discipline

8. Rejection For Right-Doing

7. Peacefulness

6. Cleanliness

5. Compassion For Others

4. Craving For Right-Doing

3. Self-Control

2. Anxious For Perfection

1. Self-Discontent

The Beatitudes
Matthew 5:3-12

Step 1 – <u>Self-Discontent</u>

Blessed are the poor in spirit: for theirs is the kingdom of heaven.

Those who want that inward beauty must first be dissatisfied with any situation in their life that does not promote a positive influence or generate positive results. *Where there is no desire for change, there will be no change.*

Step 2 – <u>Anxious for Perfection</u>

Blessed are they that mourn: for they shall be comforted.

There must be a constant yearning to improve the life. Every new day is an opportunity to be a better person, do a better deed, and achieve a better position.

Step 3 – <u>Self-Control</u>

Blessed are the meek: for they shall inherit the earth.

Personal imaging is improved by the achievement of a higher level of daily self-control, thus improving the character.

Step 4 – <u>Craving for Right-Doing</u>

Blessed are they which do hunger and thirst after righteousness: for they shall be filled.

There is no progression without a desire and a will to do those things that are right.

Step 5 – <u>Compassion for Others</u>

Blessed are the merciful: for they shall obtain mercy.

As Christ is compassionate to us, we are to demonstrate compassion to our fellow wo/man—even those who have hurt us.

Step 6 – <u>Cleanliness</u>

Blessed are the pure in heart: for they shall see God.

Those who are pure in heart are those who place pure motives behind every act or expression.

Step 7 – <u>Peacefulness</u>

Blessed are the peacemakers: for they shall be called the children of God.

In every offensive situation, focus on being the one to create harmony at any cost.

Step 8 – Accepting Rejection for Right-Doing

Blessed are they which are persecuted for righteousness' sake: for theirs is the kingdom of heaven.

Punishment for wrong-doing can be acceptable but hardly welcomed. When one suffers for right doing, this is an act of unfairness. However, in Christ, there is no greater joy than experiencing injustice as a result of standing for that which is right.

Step 9 – Discipline

Blessed are ye, when men shall revile you, and persecute you, and shall say all manner of evil against you falsely, for my sake.
Rejoice, and be exceeding glad: for great is your reward in heaven: for so persecuted they the prophets which were before you.

Discipline is endurance. Not just once, but enduring time and time again. Being able to go up the stairs, down the stairs, and back again– continually.

Decision

If upward mobility depends on inward beauty, I want a character that will take me to higher heights and completeness in Christ Jesus.

Chapter Two
Personal Imaging, Part II

The external look of a complete wo/man should be a powerful and deliberate announcement of a unique message. Like the fig tree, each of us sends a message to the world via our appearance. The message says, "Stay away from me;" or "I am approachable; I have something to give to you; I have a message to share." Your appearance is a letter to everyone you greet, or to those who only watch you from a distance.

You **are** how you look, speak, and act. The Bible records, *"for as a man thinketh in his heart, so is he"*-- Proverbs 23:7. Those with fruit, as well as leaves, possess drawing power. This power is evidenced in your *spiritual posture*, *confident imagery*, and *high-level performance*. This is what **Personal Imaging, Part II** is all about.

Spiritual Posture

Spiritual posture is a position assumed by one who knows her/his purpose in life, the mission that is to be pursued, and the wherewithal by which the task is to be accomplished. *Spiritual posture* is akin to physical posture; however, it does not matter if you are standing tall or sitting in a wheelchair, you can still exude with an all encompassing radiance.

I am reminded of a conversation I had early in my ministry. It was with the printer with whom we contracted to duplicate stationery and business cards for The Seminars. He asked, "What do you mean by **The**

Complete **Woman/Man Seminars**?" He added that he did not need a seminar to let him know he was complete. He said, "I have two hands, two feet, a brain, 10 toes, 10 fingers, etc. I am complete." What this individual was saying is that he was physically whole. However, there is a difference between physical wholeness and spiritual completeness. Whether one is physically whole or physically handicapped, s/he can **only** be complete in Christ Jesus.

Confident Imagery

Confident imagery is displayed in your attitude and your personality. It is God who supplies confident imagery--the assurance that His complete wo/man can be the same at anytime, around anyone, in any place. S/he has the ministry of presence. A presence that says, "I am complete, and I do not desire your affirmation because God has already affirmed me." Confident imagery is displayed in your handshake, your smile, and your speech. Your entire demeanor, though reserved, is spiritually uninhibited.

Good health is a very important part of _confident imagery_. Therefore, no personal imaging seminar would be complete without emphasis on care for the body. Your body is a very important part of the image you portray. How is it looking? How are you feeling? Our wise Creator has given us responsibility for the care of our physical being; and, He will not do for us those things we need to do for ourselves.

The original health plan for wo/man consisted of eight (8) essentials:

1. Fresh Air
2. Sunlight
3. Water
4. Exercise
5. The Edenic Diet – (grains, nuts, and fruits)
6. Periodic Rest
7. Abstemiousness – (limiting one's eating & drinking)
8. Abiding Trust in the Creator

The overall condition of a wo/man's body—the mental, physical, and emotional soundness—is vital to the every-day performance of duty. **A complete wo/man does not have to be in perfect health to be complete, but s/he must be able to perform perfectly within the range and scope of her/his abilities.**

High Level Performance

High-level performance is the end result of a deportment and an appearance void of human strength and filled with Divine power. The complete wo/man knows that left alone s/he has no power. "For it is God which worketh in you both to will and to do of his good pleasure"--Philippians 2:13.

I have heard some say that God is not concerned about how we look. Wo/men can look and dress according to their tastes; it is the heart that counts. After all, it is man who looks on the outward appearance.

The Complete Wo/Man: An Index to The Heart

In 1 Samuel 16:7, it is recorded, "...for man looketh on the outward appearance, but the Lord looketh on the heart." Placed in its proper context, this reference relates to the time Samuel was ordered by God to anoint a son from the house of Jesse as King Saul's successor. Samuel believed that the son God would choose was Eliab because he looked like (appeared to have all the potentials of) a king. Let us look at verses 6 and 7 of 1 Samuel chapter 16.

> *And it came to pass, when they were come, that he looked on Eliab, and said, Surely the Lord's anointed is before him.*
> *But the Lord said unto Samuel, Look not on his countenance, or on the height of his stature; because I have refused him: for the Lord seeth not as man seeth; for man looketh on the outward appearance, but the Lord looketh on the heart.*

The son Samuel anointed was Jesse's youngest, the shepherd boy, David. David, inspite of his vocation, possessed a personal imaging described in v. 12 that "was ruddy, and withal of a beautiful countenance, and goodly to look to. And the Lord said, Arise, anoint him: for this is he."

The Complete Woman/Man Seminars teaches "goodliness" of heart and modesty in appearance. Within the framework of modesty, **Personal Imaging, Part II** promotes *simplicity*, *durability*, and *versatility* in dress. Our directives are from The Master Designer.

The Master Designer

At creation, Adam and Eve had no need for material clothing. They were clothed with the righteousness of God. After wo/man sinned, the glory of God left them "and they knew that they were naked; and they sewed fig leaves together, and made themselves aprons"--Genesis 3:7. They were nude. The shame of their nakedness caused them to hide from The Creator when He came to Eden for their afternoon meeting (v.8).

After sin, Adam and Eve, immediately went "shopping" for clothes. But in the eyes of God they were not well dressed. The fig leaves did not fully cover their nakedness, protect their bodies, or honor their Maker. So, God held a complete wo/man seminar in Eden. In this **Personal Imaging, Part II** presentation, he taught the two participants how to dress well.

Genesis 3:21 records that our first parents were clothed in garments of exceptional quality: "Unto Adam also and to his wife did the Lord God make coats of skins and clothed them." Clothing of skin suggests modest covering that was *simple*, *durable*, and *versatile*.

Simplicity

Simple clothing is that which does not divert attention from the subject--YOU. If you are the messenger with the message, then a panorama of multi-colors and needless accessories is distracting, and sometimes a turn off, to the person or persons to whom you are to make that lasting impression.

- Solid colors
- Appropriate accent pieces
- Symmetry

are the goals to be reached in simplicity. The simpler and more defined your garments, the more pronounced and effective your presence.

Durability

Whether you are rich or poor, old or young, short or tall, buy quality. Buy the best that you can afford – only when you can afford it. If you don't have a lot of money, then it is going to take you longer to acquire what those with available funds may have. Why? Because you will practice deferred gratification. You will wait, and save, then purchase.

- Buy the best for less
- Select garments that can be easily maintained
- Choose material that can be cleaned over and over again and still look new and crisp

Versatility

A complete wo/man's wardrobe must be functional. Your closet needs space and organization so garments can be sorted in "occasion" order. It is not the number of garments one has that matters. It is the ability to coordinate separates and accessorize so there can be prominence and style.

Once, in a neighborhood where I worked, there was an Army and Navy Surplus Store that I passed each day. On the side of one of its walls was a sign that read, **"The clothes you need for the life you lead."** This usually kept me reminded that not everyone can dress alike. We each have different tastes, we have varied vocational disciplines, and we travel in different social circles.

However, **Personal Imaging, Part II** maintains that it does not matter where you work, what you do, or with whom you are. You can be yourself, the unique person you were created to be; and bring honor to God in your physical witness.

Decision

If God is as concerned with my outward appearance as He is with my heart, then my personal imaging must become pleasing to Him.

Chapter Three
Interpersonal Relationships

With every person you meet, a relationship is established. When you pass a stranger by the way, and acknowledge, or refuse to acknowledge, her/his presence, you have determined how you want to relate to that individual. By the way you shake a hand, hug a chest, or plant a kiss, you create an entry to, or close a door on, a relationship. Relationships can develop from brief encounters or through long-term associations. Some brief encounters can even be more memorable than long-term relationships.

One of my most memorable brief encounters took place in a check cashing store. I had gone there to send a money-gram. As I waited in line, I became conscious of another customer, an old man, observing my presence. As I was about to leave the establishment, the gentleman approached me and asked if he could say something to me. After receiving my permission, he said, "Ma'am, you sure do looks good!" His comment was not only comical but it was somewhat flattering. As I walked the three blocks back to my place of employment, the Holy Spirit whispered to me, "It is the beauty of Jesus he saw in you." Wow! What an experience! Though I have forgotten how this man looked, I will always remember this encounter.

Long-term relationships can be as pleasurable as their origin, but without good purpose they can become meaningless. Without meaningfulness, **interpersonal relationships** can be painful. I have come to understand, believe, and know that the most lasting and meaningful **interpersonal relationships** are not built on feeling, emotions, or desire, but on an individual's completeness in Christ Jesus. Without an interpersonal relationship with the Creator, it is impossible to build an unregretable relationship with another person. **There must be a vertical connection (man-with-God) before there can be a successful horizontal (man-to-man) relationship**.

A Vertical Relationship

The Complete Woman/Man Seminars wants to assure you that God is an intricate part of every complete wo/man's life. He desires to have an intimate relationship with every wo/man who wants a relationship with Him. Whatever He asks you to give up to walk with Him, He replaces with something better. Without a vertical relationship with your Creator you will not have lasting self-satisfaction that will prepare you for an equally effective joint relationship with another. So, why not work with Him in your completeness:

YOUR WORK	HIS WORK
You come to Him	He accepts you
You confess your sins to Him	He forgives you
You humble yourself	He exalts you
You shine for Him	He honors you
You deny self	He identifies your purpose
You take up your cross	He carries your burden
You follow Him	He gives you an occupation

The Complete Wo/Man: An Index to The Heart

You pray to Him	He answers your prayers
You trust Him	He rewards your faith
You obey Him	He blesses you
You lift Him up	He draws men
You surrender to Him	He repays you

Horizontal Relationships

Perhaps the most difficult of **interpersonal relationships** are those where two or more lives are intrinsically linked yet not all parties have reached the level of completeness as we have defined in this book. Domestic relationships involving husband and wife and parent and child usually fall into this category.

Many dysfunctional family relationships are caused by selfishness. It is selfish to think that your spouse, or child, should react, think, and perform within the same realm as yourself. We are all different. We are diverse culturally, generationally, and ideologically. With that understanding, each should desire to increase tolerance levels by recognizing every family member's uniqueness. In other words, allow your spouse to live her/his life according to God's design and educate your children by example.

The complete wo/man can receive Divine help when confronted with uncontrollable relational situations. In His goodness and mercy, God will protect you and give you wisdom to weather any storm in your life. The scriptures affirm that He never gives you more than you can handle:

> *There hath no temptation taken you but such as is common to man: but God is faithful, who will not suffer you to be tempted above that ye are able; but will with the temptation also make a way to escape, that ye may be able to bear it.—*
> *I Corinthians 10:13*

In every difficulty God has a way out, but you must believe and trust Him. Don't take solutions into your own hands, but trust God for His deliverance. Sometimes your answer to your problem, the thing that seems so right, is not God's solution. He can provide solutions over and beyond your imagination. Sometimes, He may send an answer contrary to what you would have wished, that may seem to hurt more than the initial problem, but as you allow time to interpret the blessing, you thank and praise God for His intervention.

Make a Change and See a Difference

In strained and distant **interpersonal relationships**, it is always the "other person" who needs to change. It is so easy to blame others for our predicament. But while the other person may be a contributor to, or even the cause of the problem, it is YOU who must change, adjust, or accept in order to maintain your completeness. This is portrayed so vividly in the Bible.

The Complete Wo/Man: An Index to The Heart

From time to time as we have addressed women's conferences, we elaborate on Bible themes to which contemporaries can relate. Of particular interest to me has been the triangular love story in the book of Genesis, chapter 29. Jacob, Leah, and Rachel are the main characters. Jacob was deceived into marrying Leah whom he did not love, but later married her sister Rachel whom he loved very dearly. Leah knew that even though she was the first wife, she was the second choice. Actually, she was not chosen at all. She was only accepted. Even though Leah was confused and damaged by lack of love from her husband, God loved her and opened her womb.

Leah believed that with the birth of their first three sons she would win the affections of her husband. In Genesis 29:32, Leah named her first child Reuben, and said, "Because the Lord has looked upon my affliction; surely now my husband will love me." But that did not happen. In verse 33, Leah named son number two Simeon, and said, "Because the Lord has heard that I am hated, he has given me this son also." But, Leah was still her husband's second best. Then in verse 34, she conceived again and named her third son Levi: "Now this time my husband will be joined to me, because I have borne him three sons."

I believe that Leah may have done some other things to try and please her husband. Knowing the heart of a woman, imagine with me that Leah patronized the lingerie stores of her day; she was hygienic; she watched her weight; and she went to the hair stylist often. Nevertheless, these and all other efforts failed to win the love of Jacob.

Like many women, Leah was trying to please a man who did not love her. She felt the pain of physical involvement without emotional attachment. One day Leah came to herself. I can imagine that she said:

> *I have looked at this picture. It seems nothing that I do pleases Jacob, not even my fertility.*
> *I have talked about him with my best friend; I have taunted my sister with my ability to have children; and I have lived with self-blame long enough.*
> *I am not going to call the pastor or* **The Complete Woman/Man Seminars** *consultants,* **I am going to praise the Lord**!

In verse 35, Leah made the best decision of her life. She said, "This time I will praise the Lord." So, she named her fourth son Judah, which means *praise*.

I can imagine that when Judah was born, his brothers: Reuben, Simeon, and Levi no longer had to watch their mother pining away in self-pity. Mama Leah had become a new woman, all because she allowed the uncontrollable circumstances of her life to dissolve in the joy of her praise.

God did not change the circumstances in Leah's life. **He readjusted HER focus from man-made happiness to Christ-centered joy**. In her new disposition, Leah was able to display the self-confident behavior of a complete woman. Her interpersonal relationship skills had improved because she placed God first in her life.

Like Leah, you may have a triangular relationship in your life. The two factions might not be a Jacob or a Rachel, but other situations that interfere with your relationship to God and with your fellow wo/man can be just as devastating as these Biblical characters faced.

This story allows me to encourage you to praise the Lord in every situation. How can you do this? By leaving **everything** in His hands and thanking Him in advance for how He will work your problem out. When a situation is too big for you to handle, you must "let go and let God." Once you give up your self-seeking efforts to solve all your problems and give God permission to use His power through your praise, He will bring joy, peace, and happiness to your life. Leah made a change in her attitude and saw a difference in her altitude.

Every Wo/Man Should Have One

God shows His love for us in many ways and through the acts of many people. One of the sure ways that He supports us in our daily struggles is through words of kindness and encouragement from friends. In our seminars we encourage participants, both women and men, to develop a meaningful interpersonal relationship with at least one person. A person you can call a friend, a spiritual friend, who will always give you good advice.

For over a quarter of a century, my girlfriend, Betty, and I have had an **interpersonal relationship**. This relationship is older than my children; it has outlasted my marriage of 23 years which ended in the death of my spouse; and it has endured the dissolution of my second marriage. Betty was with me in the initial stages of **The Complete Woman/Man Seminars'** organization, and she has worked with me through every stage of its growth. I love and appreciate my friend more than I can truly understand. I know God has placed this beautiful woman in my life as an example of His love. There are times when I get upset with my friend because she shares with me words of counsel that are not in harmony with my thinking. However, I never stay upset at her for long, because I know she is God-fearing and only wants the best for me.

On one occasion, I placed a long-distance call to Betty. I was going through a parental "crisis" and I needed so desperately to talk with someone. As the telephone rang, I prayed that Betty would be in place—no voice mail, please! When the call was received, I said, "Oh, thank God you are home!" and proceeded to explain my problem. Betty's response, "Girl, I am on my way to a meeting, and I really don't know what to tell you except, read Job 5:12-27. Then get on your knees and stay connected. Got to go, chow!" Was I ever steaming. I wanted someone to talk to. I wanted someone to join in my self-pity. I wanted my friend to care. What did I get? A referral to the scriptures. With nowhere to turn and no one to turn to, who would not put my problem on the 6:00 o'clock news, I opened the Word of God.

What a blessing! I could not believe that Job 5 had the answer to all the questions that were in my heart. After reading what God wanted me to see; after discovering the answers to my questions; and finding the solutions to my fears; I could not but fall on my knees and thank God for such a friend.

Good **interpersonal relationships** are those which help you to rise above the mundane things of life. In an interpersonal relationship that might be going sour, there is only one thing you can do. Ask God to help you accept His removal of the obstacle, His changing the heart of the other person, or His giving you strength through His power to pass the test of a relationship put in place for your learning and spiritual growth.

Decision

I want God to help me to understand that the solution to all my problems begins not with me trying to change another person but with **my** full surrender to Him so He can make a change in me.

Chapter Four
You and Your Money

We have attended and given enough financial management seminars to be weary of them. Our paradigm has become "Money Management Made Easy." When you become complete, when you have been fortified with self-control and discipline, money management is as simple as it is basic. You manage your money by doing with it what God tells you to do: return to Him a tenth; take care of your household; pay your debts; and, with the amount that remains . . .

- Invest
- Feed the hungry
- Clothe the naked
- Care for the widows and the fatherless
- Give to the poor

Everything we have, or think we own, belongs to God. The Bible records:

> *For every beast of the forest is mine, and the cattle upon a thousand hills.*
> *I know all the fowls of the mountains: and the wild beasts of the field are mine.*
> *If I were hungry, I would not tell thee; for the world is mine, and the fulness thereof.*
> *Offer unto God thanksgiving; and pay thy vows unto the most High:*
> *And call upon me in the day of trouble: I will deliver thee, and thou shalt glorify me--Psalms 50:10-12 & 14,15.*

We are all stewards of God's property and beneficiaries of His goodness and His mercy. If you have been blessed with wealth, it is because God has allowed it. If you are blessed to be poor, He wants to increase your faith in His ability to take care of you through the benevolence of those who have. God is the distributor of all wealth. He has delegated authority to the rich for their care of the poor. And these directives are found in Deuteronomy 15:7-11.

You who are rich must not hoard or boast, but remember that **you and your money are partners in construction**. You the builder, and it the tool. You are building structures of benevolence, walls of protection, doors of opportunity, and windows of hope. Anything less makes you an unworthy steward.

God has a remarkable way of redistributing wealth. If you are among the poor now, you don't have to be poor always. The "underprivileged," as the poor are defined by society, needs to stop spending precious time worrying and start trusting. If you need more trusting power, read excerpts from the Sermon on the Mount (Matthew 6:27-34):

> *Which of you by taking thought can add one cubit unto his stature?*
> *And why take ye thought for raiment? Consider the lilies of the field, how they grow; they toil not, neither do they spin:*
> *And yet I say unto you, That even Solomon in all his glory was not arrayed like one of these.*
> *Wherefore, if God so clothe the grass of the field,*

which today is, and to morrow is cast into the oven, shall he not much more clothe you, O ye of little faith?

Therefore take no thought, saying, What shall we eat? Or, What shall we drink? Or, Wherewithal shall we be clothed?

(For after all these things do the Gentiles seek:) for your heavenly Father knoweth that ye have need of all these things.

But seek ye first the kingdom of God, and his righteousness; and all these things shall be added unto you.

Take therefore no thought for the morrow: for the morrow shall take thought for the things of itself. Sufficient unto the day is the evil thereof.

All are recipients of God's love. His love for all wo/men is unconditional. But, his promises and special blessings are conditional. From the book of Genesis through Revelation, promises are almost always preceded by, "If you do... I will . . ." And He does. When funds are low in my household, I am always reminded of the scripture in Isaiah 58:13 & 14:

If thou turn away thy foot from the sabbath, from doing thy pleasure on my holy day; and call the sabbath a delight, the holy of the Lord, honourable; and shall honor him, not doing thine own ways, nor finding thine own pleasure, nor speaking thine own words:

Then shalt thou delight thyself in the Lord; and I will cause thee to ride upon the high places of the *earth, **and feed thee with the heritage of Jacob thy father:** for the mouth of the Lord hath spoken it.*

God does not take pleasure in deprivation, hardship, and sorrow. He takes pleasure in obedience. The promise here is if we obey, God will *feed* us with the heritage of Jacob our father. He did not say He would give to us Jacob's heritage, but that he would *feed* us with it. If we will obey Him, we shall prosper. God honors our obedience with fulfilled promises. Trust in God and obedience to His word, create a financial comfort zone that every complete wo/man occupies. Consequently, s/he is not overly concerned about developing a business relationship with the bank manager, but with the account holder. The one who makes the deposits and authorizes the withdrawals—our Father.

Money management at its best is understanding the Source from which the funds come, and your responsibility as custodian. Yes. You did earn it.

But thou shalt remember the Lord thy God: for it is he that giveth thee power to get wealth that he may establish his covenant which he sware unto thy fathers as it is this day-- Deuteronomy 8:18.

Whether you receive a pension, a wage, or an inheritance, it all begins with God and His power of distribution. However, it ends with you and your acknowledgment of His ownership.

The Complete Wo/Man: An Index to The Heart

The Complete Woman/Man Seminars cannot tell you how to spend your money; but we can offer guidance on how to wisely appropriate that which our all knowing Creator has entrusted you.

Decision

God creates, owns, and distributes wealth; therefore, I will be a worry-free financial custodian.

Chapter Five
The Complete Woman

The Complete Woman/Man Seminars, at its inception, addressed only needs of women. We thought, and still do think, that if women were empowered to be all that they can be through enlightenment, then manhood and/or fatherhood would be lifted to higher levels of completeness. Thereby, improving the quality of family life in each individual family unit.

I have come to know that problems of womanhood do not perpetuate because of disobedient children, unfaithful husbands, or deadbeat dads. These may all be causes for a woman to readjust her lifestyle, but they are not causative factors for low self-esteem, self-pity, or self-imposed limitations. If women are to survive the onslaught of oppression, they must obtain freedom from sin and the stupor in which sin places them. It is time for women to move from silliness to seriousness. The scriptures talk about "silly" women in II Timothy 3:1-7:

> *This know also, that in the last days perilous times shall come.*
> *For men shall be lovers of their own selves, covetous, boasters, proud, blasphemers, disobedient to parents, unthankful, unholy.*
> *Without natural affection, trucebreakers, false accusers, incontinent, fierce, despisers of those that are good,*
> *Traitors, heady, highminded, lovers of pleasures more than lovers of God;*
> *Having a form of godliness, but denying the power thereof; from such turn away.*

*For of this sort are they which creep into houses, and lead captive **silly** women laden with sins, led away with divers lusts,*
Ever learning, and never able to come to the knowledge of truth.

By identifying personal worth through the eyes of God, women are enabled to perform at their fullest capability, to be an example to others, and to treat fellow women and men with respect. It is now time for women to look at life's seeming barriers, impediments, and boundaries as stepping-stones to a better life. In the process of stepping up, the complete woman announces, "This is who I am. This is what I think of myself. And, this is how I expect to be treated."

God's Complete Woman is . . .

SPIRITUAL

- She is confident in her relationship with The Creator knowing that without Him survival itself is impossible.

PROFESSIONAL AND PERSONAL

- She looks her best in all circumstances and seeks to make others feel at ease around her.

- She adapts to changes in her environment without apparent difficulty.

- She is always prepared to override those factors that illuminate her imperfections.

The Complete Wo/Man: An Index to The Heart

MORAL

- She accepts responsibility for her own actions.

- She is trustworthy and confidential.

- She realizes that it is all right to make mistakes and that it is stylish to apologize.

WISE

- She continually strives for self-improvement through the acquisition of knowledge.

- She **R-E-A-D-S** (inspirational, political, social, and economic literature).

COMMITTED

- She is committed to God, to family, to friends, and to herself.

FOCUSED

- She concentrates, daily, on things that make her life happy, fulfilling, and rewarding.

Marcia B. Armstead

She is Spiritual

When a woman becomes serious about life, she learns that her first step to an improved existence is to worship God. Once I was asked to give a keynote address for a Family Life program. As always, I asked God to show me a family in the Bible that exemplified quality family life. He directed me to the book of I Samuel, Chapter One. In that chapter was not only examples of family life with its ups and downs, but I became acquainted with one of the most complete women in history. Her name is Hannah.

Commencing the 55 chapters in the books of First and Second Samuel is an elaborate account of the circumstances surrounding the preconception of Samuel. Even though Samuel is the most important character in the opening portion of the books, his mother, Hannah, takes center stage.

Hannah is one of the few Old Testament mothers who received honorable mention in the Bible. Her profound presence and importance was the prelude to Samuel's greatness. Even though she was a wife, favored by her husband, Elkanah, in the eyes of society, and to herself as well, her womanhood was incomplete because "the Lord had shut up her womb" (v. 5).

It might have been personal shame, social embarrassment, and constant domestic mockery (v. 6) that compelled her to pray unreservedly to be blessed by God with fertility. And, perhaps her deep emotional turmoil was understood best by other barren Hebrew women. Hannah, however, knew that her refuge was in worship. Beneath the stigma of her childlessness, she uttered a desperate, passionate plea to God for the help that only He could give. Hannah prayed for a baby. God honored her request and promised to grant her petition.

The same intense faith with which Hannah sought the help of God in her life continued between the petition and the fulfilled promise of a man-child. **Between the petition and the promise**, Hannah recognized that there was One who loved her more than any human being and who was able and willing to bless her by removing her inability to conceive. During the prenatal stages of Hannah's experience, she held steadfast trust in a prayer-answering God; One who cared about every intimate fiber of her being and directed her through the preparatory stages of motherhood. The mother of Samuel maintained her complete surrender to God's will. It was her unwavering commitment to the God of Israel that allowed her to keep her vow of dedicating Samuel to the service of the Lord (v. 11) for a lifetime.

It would be unfair to applaud Hannah without recognizing that she had a husband with a God-fearing spirit. Hannah's devotion to God was not a threat to the monarch of the home. Her vow did not diminish the quality of their family life. Elkanah's devotion to God, his love for Hannah, and his keen acknowledgment of Hannah's relationship with God enabled Him to render unselfish support to his wife (v. 23).

Like Hannah, the greatest testimony any woman can give is a portrayal of her relationship with the Creator. Any woman who wants to develop a lasting (eternal) relationship with God, must worship as did Hannah:

persistently when the odds are against you; wholeheartedly, when no one but God can help you; diligently, returning to Him whatever He asks, and whatever you have promised. **Between the petition and the promise is the safest, surest, and happiest place to be with God.**

She is Professional and Personal

A professional woman embraces life with the strengths and abilities she has been afforded to make a difference in the world. Being professional and personal means she has made a conscious decision to be a winner. She realizes she cannot run through the arena of life for a significant other, nor can a loved one pave the pathway for her, but she can make adjustments, in any situation, to be an asset and not a liability.

I had the privilege a few years ago to meet a professional and personal woman named Carmel. Before Carmel was married, she lived a very fulfilled single life. One day as we talked about some of her accomplishments, I was in awe at the things she had done during her years as a single woman: she ran her own business, she was independent, and totally satisfied with life. What was more amazing is that even though she had made some adjustments to include a husband in her life, her ideals and pursuits encountered no submersion. Her marriage was very cohesive, and she had been blessed with a very special man. She was gleeful and happy as she talked about her past and her present. I remember my comment, "Wow! You are such a complete woman."

Her response, "If you think I am complete now, then I guess I always have been."

Carmel has been professional and personal in my presence and among the other colleagues with whom we have associated. One thing I remember most about her adjustment from single life to married life is that she made a deliberate attempt to change her hairstyle from one requiring high maintenance to a style that was always "good to go." This was in order that she could travel with her husband at a moment's notice. Her personal life did not hamper, but rather complemented her professional life and that of her husband's.

A professional and personal woman will always be a winner especially when she surrenders her life to the will of God. As a Christian, she may not always be understood or accepted "[for] the natural man receiveth not the things of the Spirit of God: for they are foolishness unto him: neither can he know them, because they are spiritually discerned" (I Corinthians 2:14). However, a life that has definition and purpose will always leave an impression on observers and service recipients.

She is Moral

Morality is the act of making choices. The ability to make decisions between right and wrong. Woman was created with the ability to choose. This is the greatest power she was ever given. How she exercises that power determines her morality.

A moral woman must be honest enough to accept responsibility for her own actions. Accepting responsibility is not the same as self-blame. It is acknowledging that a mistake was made that she could have prevented someone from making, or that she could have avoided herself.

About thirty months into my widowhood, I met a man who, seriously, wanted to marry me. During an early telephone conversation, he made the following comment, "If we were married, you would really make me look good, and I want to marry a woman who will help me keep my hands in God's hands." Antennas went up. Why? Because I knew no woman could quench the hunger of a person's heart. That is God's gift to the person who is searching. Well, I married that man, for what I thought were all the "right" reasons (love, intimacy, maintenance), and the re-marriage failed.

After a period of self-consultation, I accepted responsibility for not trusting God enough to believe He could, and can, take care of **all** *my* needs. I have learned that **God taking away the desire for a want is just the same as satisfying the need**. A moral woman knows that in God's marital equation ONE + ONE = ONE; and that a happy and successful marriage is not made up of two halves. It is composed of two complete persons who have decided to unite their lives for big business and have registered to be of service to God, help to their fellow wo/man, and encouragement to one another.

A complete woman does not need a husband to complete or satisfy her. (That is God's work.) But, a spouse can encourage her in her ambitions, support her self-improvement efforts, and applaud her for the success she has made of her life, and this works both ways.

She is Wise

Wisdom, the ability to follow the soundest course of action, is what makes a woman steadfast in her spiritual, professional, and moral stature. Wise decisions keep you elevated and admired. Wisdom not only steers you away from duplicating an error, it shows you how to intelligently pull yourself out of a rut.

One of the worse situations a woman can find herself in is an abusive domestic relationship. The most tragic domestic abusive situation I have ever witnessed was not a battering, a killing, or an eviction. I have read about, heard about, or witnessed all of these. I do, however, have vivid recall of one day visiting a medical center in a certain city. As I sat in the waiting area along side a mother and her four-year-old child, this "baby" began to call his mother some of the most derogatory four and five-letter words I had ever heard from the lips of a child. Mom kept saying, "Stop saying that!" And, her son just laughed as he continued the name-calling. The child did not know the meaning of those words. It was evident that he was expressing what he had heard someone else say to his mother.

I believe a woman can experience no greater emotional injury than verbal abuse from the man she loves. There are three responsive behaviors to hurting words that some women have taken:

(1) Some respond in kind, putting themselves on the same level as the abuser,

39

Marcia B. Armstead

(2) Many women accept the abuse and become enablers to the recurrences,

(3) There are those who simply will not stand to be degraded by any man--verbally or otherwise-- and will aid in terminating the pattern of abuse.

How you respond to abusive situations is indicative of your level of self-esteem and your spiritual awareness of who and Whose you are.

Would Jesus, the Son of God, our Saviour and Lord call us names? Many women would say, "No way!" Not the most passionate, sensitive man who ever walked the earth. Not the one who promoted, uplifted, and liberated the women of the New Testament. Jesus? Abusive? Never!

The Canaanite woman of **Matthew 15** begs to differ. It was this same Jesus who called her, and her people, "dogs" (v 26). She had come to Him because her family life was shattered. She lived with a daughter who was devil possessed and she had come to worship Jesus by requesting healing for her child. Her daughter had probably called her every vile name possible; made it unbearable for her to live in her own home; and created numerous problems in their neighborhood.

This woman came to the ultimate Source of help— Jesus, and His response was: "It is not meet to take the children's bread, and to cast it to dogs" (v 26). What a slap in the face; what a direct attack at her self-esteem; what a hit below the belt! Her daring response to Jesus in v. 27 "... yet the dogs eat of the crumbs which fall from

Chapter Six
The Complete Man

What completes a man is essentially that which makes a woman complete—an interpersonal relationship with God. However, there are mandates given to man by God that were, and are, not applicable to woman. Man's completeness differs in *his role*, *his responsibility*, and *his activities*.

In the Book of Genesis, Chapter 2, is the creation story of God's provision for Adam. He prepared **a home** for the first man; it was the Garden of Eden (vs. 8):

> And the Lord God planted a garden eastward in Eden; and there he put the man whom he had formed.

He gave him **a career**--an agricultural occupation of dressing the garden (vs.15):

> And the Lord God took the man, and put him into the garden of Eden to dress it and to keep it.

God also gave Adam **environmental boundaries** (vs.16 & 17):

> And the Lord God commanded the man saying, Of every tree of the garden thou mayest freely eat:
> But of the tree of the knowledge of good and evil, thou shalt not eat of it: for in the day that thou eatest thereof thou shalt surely die.

Adam had a home, a job, and a consciousness of God's presence, **before** God gave him a woman. Genesis chapter 2: 18 states, "And the Lord God said, It is not good that the man should be alone; I will make him an help meet for him." **The woman was a special creature, not only because God made her so beautiful, but because Adam had the capacity to admire, love, and appreciate her**.

Before sin, our first family exemplified the type of lifestyle God wants each complete family to model. Woman was to complement man by fulfilling his completeness, and their children were to be taught obedience to God and adherence to the laws of nature. **After sin**, our first family was much the same as most families today. There was in the Edenic home disobedience to God's will, waywardness, and disloyalty. As a result, the family of Adam and Eve became as dysfunctional as many are today.

The plan of salvation is to restore man to the quality of family life before sin's entry. **The Complete Woman/Man Seminars** endeavors to assist men in establishing, or re-establishing, their personal foothold in the "quicksand" of lost title, forfeited authority, and relinquished responsibilities. Thus, in our seminars, we focus on oppositions that prevent man from reaching completeness and on elements of restoration to full duties of manhood.

His Role

The *role* of a man is the essence of his existence. He is the leader, the head of the home, the provider, and the lover. His role and influence can be destroyed, misunderstood, or abused. **One** of the most destructive forces of manhood is self-destruction, brought on by his yielding to unholy, immoral influences. Satan is the master deceiver, who studies and knows man's weaknesses. He uses these to lead men into making wrong choices. Consequently, he can disable an entire family by weakening the man.

The scriptures in Matthew, Chapter 12:29, states, "Or else how can one enter into a strong man's house, and spoil his goods, except he first bind the strong man? and then he will spoil his house."

Self-destruction, yielding to sin and its consequences, not only harms you, but similarly affects those who love and depend on you. Your indiscrete actions can induce the resentment of immediate family members and the disappointment of parents. When others cannot depend on your performance because of personal failure(s), they, consciously or subconsciously, begin to strip you of your authority as a role model.

A second way man loses his superior role is by deliberate domestic assault brought on by the over-expectations of others. Some women expect more from a man than he can actually give while doing very little to help or support him. Consequently, no matter what he does it is never enough. His manhood is attacked even further when shown constant disrespect by those he loves. But, a complete man accepts responsibility for the part he might have played to trigger the behavior and moves on.

You survive the offender's darts by removing self and viewing the other person as the one to be helped. While a state of selflessness is not easy to attain, men must bury pride and put egos to sleep in order to move forward.

Thirdly, society condemns some men by stereotyping them or keeping them bound and shackled in an inescapable gravel pit. Just one mistake, one immoral decision, can turn a rich man into a pauper, a poor man into a beggar, and an educated man into a wayfarer. It is a travesty to watch the penalties imposed on law-breakers. Once you have been labeled, you can wear that stigma for a lifetime. Getting back to the level of society's standards can be very difficult. There are usually no stairs back to the top, and sometimes when you do make it to the top, your climb has been a landslide struggle.

Any occurrence that circumvents the God-given authority of a man renders him incapable of fulfilling his completeness. But, whether a man has lost his position through self-destruction, domestic mutiny, or public sabotage, he can regain and maintain his manhood, because the One who makes you complete is not condemning, but forgiving.

His Responsibility

A complete man is first, and foremost, spiritual--he walks with God. If he is a husband, he is the priest of his home, he loves his wife, and loves and corrects his children. All other responsibilities are secondary.

From time to time, in our seminars, men have exclaimed that it is becoming increasingly difficult to ascertain what women expect from men. We are often asked by men, "What does a woman want her man to be?" Our answer usually is, "If you are living up to what God wants you to be, then a complete woman's expectation is relatively **S.I.M.P.L.E.**" A complete woman wants her complete man to be:

- **S** piritual

- **I** ntelligent

- **M** ature

- **P** rofessional

- **L** oveable

- **E** ncouraging

How a man fulfills these expectations demonstrates how well he has accepted this unique challenge and how willing he is to be God's man and a man for all seasons.

My friend, Audrey, is married to a complete, and **S.I.M.P.L.E.**, man. Audrey is psychologically, educationally, financially, and physically independent. Among the many enormous challenges she has embraced is the establishment and administration of an educational training center that produces gifted children. Audrey's assertiveness would probably be a threat to any ordinary man, but she is married to a very extraordinary gentleman who stands taller than any man I know because he truly knows how to serve his woman, and accept her unique gifts.

I mention Audrey because her definition of a complete man is unique. On numerous occasions I have heard her say, "I do not need a man to put food on my table, clothes on my back, or shelter over my head. I married a man who knows how to treat me like a queen and keep me on a pedestal." Then she adds, "When my husband ceases to do that, then he has failed in his purpose–and I will no longer need him." Quite crude, but very honest. The greatest part of a complete man's *responsibility* is serving a woman unselfishly and with dignity.

A complete man demonstrates to his sons how to be men and teaches his daughters to relate to males. Your *responsibility* as a man is to **show** your son, or someone else's son, how to be a man: how to respect a woman, how to develop good work ethics; how to maintain integrity. This knowledge has to be seen in your day-to-day performance. Sure, there are complete men who have been raised by women, but, generally speaking, only a man can show a boy how to be a man.

Every father should have a trusting relationship with his daughter. You cannot show her how to be a woman, but you can be an example of the man she does or does not want to marry. You are the one who can make your daughter feel like a princess by being attentive to her personal imaging and her conduct. Give her constructive criticism, encouragement, and compliments as needed. Never allow another man to tell her what she should have heard from you.

The Complete Wo/Man: An Index to The Heart

The *responsibilities* of a complete man may appear overwhelming at times, but any neglect of duty when it is within your power to perform, destroys confidence in you and your delegated authority from your Maker.

His Activities

The *activities* of a man--that which occupies his time, captures his devotion, and controls his involvement—are what define him. The complete man displays his true worth in how he protects, directs, and associates with his family. Leadership at home prepares him, and other family members, to be viable contributors to society.

One of the most fascinating men in Old Testament scripture is David the son of Jesse. We talked about David in **Chapter Two**, but he is worth mentioning again. David was a shepherd boy, a decorated soldier, a charismatic musician, a sincere friend, a devoted father, a romantic husband, and a king. He was famous not only because of these positions but because of his performance as a leader. Throughout his life, David's early childhood education dictated his behavior.

As a child, I was fascinated with the story of David and Goliath (1 Samuel 17). I always wondered why David took five stones in his satchel to fight the giant. **Why five stones when God knew David only needed one to claim victory**. It was in my adult life that the Holy Spirit impressed upon my mind the meaning of the stones:

The stones were David's gifts and talents. They were the credentials that made up his resume:

Stone #1 - was the stone of attitude/motive
Stone #2 - was David's appearance
Stone #3 - was his education
Stone #4 - his occupation
Stone #5 - was his faith

King Saul was impressed by David's resume, and after only one interview, David was hired. He was inducted into Israel's army.

Attitude/ Motive

David had good work ethics. He came for his interview in the interest of making a contribution to the company, not to see how he could goof off on the employer's time. He gave his best without concern for benefits.

Appearance

David's appearance might not have pleased the King, but he (David) knew he performed best in the clothes that fit his station in life. He could not go to battle in King Saul's armor. He was not a king. So, David wore the "uniform" of a shepherd.

The Complete Wo/Man: An Index to The Heart

Education

David's father was his teacher. Jesse, no doubt, taught him to fear and honor the God of heaven. This knowledge gave him zeal and confidence as a problem solver.

Occupation

David's previous work experience and accomplishments prepared him for his mission. He had killed a bear and a lion to protect his father's flock of sheep. He was well suited for this new occupation. And, his "user friendly" equipment – a slingshot and some stones—were all that he needed to do the job.

Faith

Most of all, David had a personal relationship with God that no one could take away. It was this dependence on God that propelled him in his task. I believe the stone of faith killed the giant Goliath.

Like the story of David and Goliath, there are major crises that come about in our lives. Some are private; some are public. But, a crisis may bring into clear and bold expression the reserve that governs a complete man's life.

Every complete man has the privilege and opportunity to package the same five stones carried by David to battle: pure motives, appropriate dress, education, occupation, and faith. In your activities, in your preparation for battle, a personal relationship with God is paramount. David's five stones are indicative of human effort exercised under the influence of God's power.

Even though David sinned, as we all have, he found his way back into the presence of God. The complete man is one who knows how to find his five stones, position himself for usefulness, and submit to God's guidance in his life.

Decision

I may not have been the complete man I should have, but, like David, please, Lord, make me a man after your own heart.

The C.P.R. of Singleness

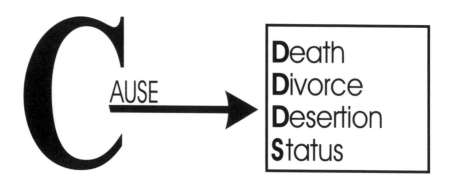

CAUSE →

> **D**eath
> **D**ivorce
> **D**esertion
> **S**tatus

PSYCHOLOGICAL RESPONSES →

> **D**enial
> **R**ejection
> **I**ndifference
> **N**eglect
> **K**nocked Down

RECOVERY →

> **W**ealth
> **A**gility
> **T**enderness
> **E**nthusiasm
> **R**estoration

Chapter Seven
Happily Unmarried

A few months after entering widowhood, my girlfriend, Betty, said to me, that perhaps God wanted me now to add a ministry for singles to our list of seminar subjects. It seemed then, that these words were the worst things she could have said to me. I was very resentful of that statement because I did not want to be single. Still in a state of denial, and wanting so badly to be married, I could not concede to ever accepting singleness as a gift. But, as usual, Betty was right. After getting past a six-month "mourning" period, God led me—very joyously— into designing a ministry for singles.

I am thankful that my friends and consultants were there to encourage this phase of our program and that single people took time out to attend our singles presentations and were blessed by them. Even after my remarriage, the singles presentation was one we thoroughly enjoyed doing and continued to do. In study and preparation for our first singles seminar, the Holy Spirit directed me to focus on **"The C.P.R. of Singleness:"** *Cause*, *Psychological Responses*, and *Recovery*. This was something entirely new to me, so I asked God to show me how to develop this concept and He did.

Cause

I was shown that there are four elements of singleness that **The Complete Woman/Man Seminars** must address.

They are:

- **D** eath
- **D** ivorce
- **D** esertion
- **S** tatus

Death, **divorce**, and **desertion** all announce the ending of a marital relationship. And those who never married are the **status** singles.

Being separated by any of the three-D's can be very devastating. There is nothing that more rapidly changes life's directions and increases (or decreases) pressures than a change in relationship status. But, the first conscious recognition is you must become a survivor.

Death. The finality of death induces more pain and hurt than any other element of separation. Yet those feelings need not linger throughout the duration of your life. As one who has experienced the death of a spouse, I know that with time for mending and healing these feelings do go away. There are some who may welcome death of a spouse, because that occurrence is the answer to a deep-rooted problem. But, whether one experiences an immediate blessing or a long-term blessing, there can be blessings in death. It took years for me to recognize blessings in my late husband's death. And even now, I am sure all the blessings have not fully been accepted, but I do know that God allowed him to pass away.

Divorce. Before the dissolution of my second marriage, I had given many singles presentations, but was unable to adequately address questions about divorce.

I did not believe in it, and could not advise anyone on how to handle herself/himself through the ordeal. But this seemingly "bad" experience in my life has turned out to be a rich blessing, and has taught me many things about the subject. I believe, however, that the most important revelation is that victims of marital breakups are not just the child/children but also the spouse who never wanted the dissolution. I thank God that I have gone through the emotions of it all and that He has used it to help me help others.

Desertion *is* an indefinite separation that usually creates more problems than it solves. Similar to its counterparts, death and divorce, this too is a passing away of an institution that used to be, could have been, and now is not. Someone did not try hard enough; someone gave up too quickly; or someone took the "easy" way out. My friend, Ruth, often shares with me adages of her late grandmother. One of the sayings that comes to mind is, "Marriage is not always 50/50. Sometimes it is 70/30; and, this off balancing might not last forever, but it fills in the gap."

Married and living single can be a putrefying process that receives no burial or decree - just a suspended sentence. As time and distance widen the separation gap, emotional, psychological, and physical "calluses" develop. It is an awkward and unfortunate position that millions of people face. Nevertheless, *desertion is* a school from which a complete wo/man can graduate.

Status singles, the never married, go through life with a contentment, an anticipation, and a degree of naivete that those who are, or were, married do not possess. Some singles who want to get married are relatively unprepared. They are, as my single friend, Chuck, once stated, "Bringing nothing to the table but a warm body and unrealistic demands."

It used to be that finding a "rich" man to marry was paramount to a woman. Now, men also look for a woman who has money. Once women looked for a man with a college degree; now some men prefer a woman with a degree or an occupation that will make her a viable wage earner. There are men who are threatened by a woman's ability to earn a comparable salary, but today's complete man is looking for a complete woman who together, with him, can create an atmosphere of financial balance and stability.

While it is good that men and women concern themselves with the ability to acquire material resources and wealth, this should not dispense with a quest for a partner with integrity. A good character is of greater value to a relationship than the balance in a savings account. The integrity of a wo/man determines not only how long the relationship will last but how well material gains will be received, preserved, and distributed.

Questions to be asked when a relationship appears to be getting serious should not only be, "Can he support me so I won't have to work?" But, "Will she value her self-worth enough to always respect me?" Not only, "Is s/he a good lover?" But, "Is s/he capable of being a good parent to our children?"

However, before one can successfully assess the present and potential responsive behaviors of another, s/he must first examine herself/himself. Each must determine what s/he will *bring to the table* in order to be a valuable part of the union. Will it be education, wealth, consistency, unselfishness, a healthy body, creativity, and/or a strong determination to maintain the marriage vows in the "better" and in the "worse" of times?

To the altar you come as you are, to be all that you can be, in a relationship that needs all that you have. Whatever each brings to the table should, at its least, equate to an intangible value system and uncompromising integrity.

Psychological Responses

Psychological responses to a marital status that you did not invite or can barely tolerate may drive you to **D.R.I.N.K.**:

- **D** enial
- **R** ejection
- **I** ndifference
- **N** eglect
- **K** nocked Down

Denial. Denying that a single life is your fortune might force you to take measures you never thought you would in order to hold on to a fragmented or improper union. Holding on to pieces will cause you to fall much harder than if you had simply let go and allowed God to settle you in His way.

Rejection. Feeling rejected is a natural emotion that the "victim" of a separation encounters. However, when you begin to see yourself as a **victor** instead of the **victim**, it makes your inevitable transition from dependence to independence a lot easier. When you recognize rejection, accept the emotion as normal, and deal with it in a rational manner, you will overcome more rapidly the overwhelming effects of the rebuff.

Indifference to your situation might be shown by children, friends, supporters and well-wishers. You may not know how to relate to them either, and communication difficulties may arise. For example, if you are widowed, divorced, or separated, your children might not know how to relate when one parent is missing. Your friends and neighbors might not know just what to say, and sometimes they will say the wrong thing. Psychologically, you deal not only with your own emotions and personal responses, but you also must contend with the responses of others toward you.

Neglect is another emotion that must be dealt with. When you feel neglected, just think of what the other person left behind and not what you have lost. What you have is many times all you need, but you must be able to see the true value in your self-worth and your importance to God. If children are involved, they too will feel the crush of neglect. But there are coping skills that they too must develop. They must be taught by your example that **ONE is a whole number** and that they are still a vital part of God's rainbow package.

The *knocked-down* feeling is the emotion that arises when you believe you have been kicked to the curb. This is the stage where you ask, "Why, why, why?"

But don't allow this emotion to carry you away into the depths of self-pity and low self-esteem. Get up; brush yourself off; and re-familiarize yourself with the unique person you are. Take note of the contributions you can and will be able to make to society. The complete wo/man can and must survive.

Recovery

There is no survival without recovery. You must be willing to move away from the past and embrace the future with determination. Recovery is necessary in order for you to progress.

Wo/men suffering from "poor me" syndromes have been heard to say, "I need a drink!" If you must drink, drink **W.A.T.E.R**.

The water that God provides is refreshing for the soul:

- **W** ealth
- **A** gility
- **T** enderness
- **E** nthusiasm
- **R** estoration

Wealth. When I think of singleness, I think of wealth--wealth of time, wealth of independent decision-making, wealth of solitary relaxation. There is something about feeling wealthy that makes you want to just be happy all the time. Wealth, as described in **Chapter Four**, is not always having money. It is knowing that when God has freed you to accept His leading in your life,

He becomes sole provider. You know that whatever the need, God has already made provisions for you.

I take this opportunity to tell single wo/men who are struggling financially that they do not have to compromise their dignity to receive or maintain support. Widowhood and its financial hardships truly strengthened my relationship with God. I discovered, beyond the shadow of a doubt, God does (and always will) supply my every need. There are myriad examples that I could give of how God has kept me in wealth. But, I will share just this one.

It was a Friday morning. I was desperately in need of $100.00. So, I prayed and asked God to shower me with just enough wealth to take a short weekend trip. After my prayer, I knew the money would come, but I did not know how. That afternoon, as I went to my mailbox, instead of the usual "junk" mail, I retrieved four envelopes that appeared to contain greeting cards. It was the month of June, not May, so I knew Mother's Day had passed. Fathers' Day was this weekend, but I am not a father. Anxious to see if a practical joke was being played, I went into my villa to open the mail. The first card said, "Happy Birthday!" I had been so absorbed with my financial need, I had forgotten that my birthday was right after Fathers' Day. When the cards had all been opened, I had received a total of $95.00 in gifts from different members of one family (Fannie, her husband, and three of their children). Oh, I praised and thanked God for answering my prayer while wondering why He had shorted me $5.00.

Happy to have received these funds, I proceeded with my out-of-town plans. The cards were placed in an appropriate area of the living room. I had planned, as I had been taught, to acknowledge receipt of these presents. I would do so after the weekend. The next week, as I sat at my desk with "Thank You" notes in hand, and re-reading the cards that I had gone through so hurriedly, a $5.00 bill fell from the last card. What a joy! Not so much that I now had money for postage stamps, but that God had truly sent me $100.00 on the day that I asked.

Money or no money; property or no property; when God is in charge of your life, just "Ask, and it shall be given you; seek, and ye shall find; knock, and it shall be opened unto you"—Matthew 7:7. Singles are wealthy wo/men when complete in Christ Jesus.

Agility is one of the best ways you can praise God for your singleness. Freedom of movement; the ability to awaken at any hour and fulfill any desire without disturbing someone else, have someone interrupt your performance, or having another person impede your progress. You have more time for exercise, for study, and for travel. Most of all, you have the autonomy to just be yourself.

Tenderness. When you have been through a difficult experience, and understand the impact, the healing process, and the end result, you can be more empathetic to others. You now know what to say and what not to say to your fellow wo/man. Your comments are appropriate, your non-verbal communication is in season, and your good deeds are punctual.

Enthusiasm is a passion for life. It is a must if you are to wake up every day feeling **"Happily Unmarried."** Being single with a purpose—a mission, a project, an assignment—is the most exciting challenge of single life. Enthusiasm is a God-given energy a complete wo/man should always have.

Restoration, complete healing, is achieved through forgiveness and understanding. While granting forgiveness might not free the person who has offended or hurt you, it releases **you**, and enables **you** to live a healthier and happier life. Many wo/men going through hardships in life seek counseling. For me, the best restorative counseling was in reading the scriptures.

When my remarriage failed, I needed clear and precise direction. I needed some wise counsel from an impartial source. I knew my answer was in the Bible, but I did not want to read it. Actually, I did not know where to turn in the Bible to get the answers I needed. So, the Holy Spirit, early one morning, escorted me through the Book of Ephesians. I read non-stop all six chapters. Chapters five and six focused on family life, Christian duties, and the Christian's armour. I cannot exactly tell you why or how this was all the therapy I needed. But, at the end of the reading, I had completely **mended** from my psychological malfunctioning.

Healing and full restoration came later in a dream.

The Dream

In my dream, I saw a big fish in a large body of water. As I looked at the moving figure, I strained as I watched it disappear around a large rock. That was the entire visual. Then, I was instructed on the meaning of this dream. The fish, the Holy Spirit said, was as the fish in whose belly Jonah had an unforgettable three-day experience with God. I was reminded that God allowed Jonah to be regurgitated without even a broken fingernail, and he immediately proceeded with the mission God had for him. The application for me was that God had me to be swallowed up in a three-year marriage that was for the most part good for my learning. I came out without any injury, still equipped with all the talents God had given me; therefore, I needed to move forward with the mission of *The Complete Woman/Man Seminars* and forget about the destination of the fish.

How God speaks to me, and how He communicates with other wo/men depends on the relationship each has established with Him. I only know that God has made me a **"Happily Unmarried"** single. One who has been married, widowed, remarried, **and** divorced. The experiences of each status have helped me to be of greater service to my fellow wo/men. Being **"Happily Unmarried"** is knowing and accepting the equation of singleness: ONE – ONE + ONE = ONE.

Your choice to be single or married is not as important as knowing that God has a blessed purpose for your life. And, wherever you find yourself right now, God is your rescue, and you must ask Him to direct your steps. But, do not force Him to place you in a situation you do not need or for which you are not prepared, because He loves you too much to withhold from you what you so desperately desire. You must trust Him enough to rest in Him and believe that He knows what is best for your life.

In closing, I want to tell you about another friend, a very important person in my life. Her name is Ivory. Ivory is able to make me laugh at the most earth-shaking experiences in my life. When "bad" things happen to me, she laughs out loud with such joy in her laughter. I tell her that I am always amazed at her responses to my unfortunate circumstances. But, she just keeps laughing, and with a glow on her face she will say, "Marcia, God is about to do something for you through this experience that is so glorious you cannot begin to imagine." And then she will add, quite solemnly, "Just stand still and see the salvation of the Lord. Rest in Him."

Oh, my friend, I want to admonish you, as Ivory has done for me. Rest in the Lord and see His salvation in your life. Let Him fill the void that keeps you from being a complete wo/man. **He has the power; but you must give Him the permission**. Jesus says, "But seek ye first the kingdom of God, and his righteousness; and all these things shall be added unto you"—Matthew 6:33. What things? You will never know until you seek Him first.

Decision
If it is healthy and complete to be **"Happily Unmarried,"** then I want to begin a single lifestyle of joy and purpose.

About the Author

Marcia Beverly Armstead is founder and president of The Complete Woman/Man Seminars. She authors, designs, and conducts group seminars leading men and women to discover their strengths and the Power Source behind those strengths.

Her aim is to help improve the spiritual, psychosocial, and physical quality of the lives of the people she addresses. In so doing, she hopes to enable each person to exercise a positive influence in the home, the work place, and in society.

Her manuscript, <u>The Complete Wo/Man: An Index to The Heart</u> is her first book of inspiration, but she has written several motivational free lance articles. Among her published work is, "Entering the Work Force: A Challenge for Women of the '90's" published by *Job Watch*, an Orlando, Florida business magazine. She is also contributor of two commentary articles for the <u>Women of Color Study Bible</u>, a 2000 publication by Nia Publishing, Atlanta, Georgia; and she is scriptwriter and producer for a Resolution Trust Corporation employee training video.

Marcia Beverly Armstead is profiled in the 1995-96 edition of <u>Marquis Who's Who of American Women</u>.

Ms. Armstead's first marriage to the late Pastor Eugene Armstead, Sr. lasted 23 years. After three years of widowhood, she remarried. Her remarriage, which lasted three years, ended in dissolution. Marcia is now happily unmarried, the mother of two sons, and grandmother of one grandson.

She describes herself as "a fully surrendered, totally committed servant of the living God." This awareness propels her in her ministry to all people.

The Formula for Success

PHIL. 4:11-13

Formula for Success

We, The Complete Woman/Man Seminars, have adopted as our formula for success that which worked so well for the Apostle Paul as found in Philippians 4:11–13:

> *Not that I speak in respect of want: for I have learned, in whatsoever state I am, therewith to be content* **[ATTITUDE]**.

> *I know both how to be abased, and I know how to abound* **[SKILL]**: *every where and in all things I am instructed both to be full and to be hungry, both to abound and to suffer need* **[EDUCATION]**.

> *I can do all things through Christ which strengtheneth me* **[SUCCESS]**.

Every complete wo/man must have a good attitude; develop skill; and pursue education. When all three are committed to God for His use, and His blessing, then true, lasting success is yours forever.

This is a theory that has been tried and proven. It worked for Paul, is has worked for us, and it will work for you.

God bless you, my friend!

Maria Armstead